U.S.A. TRAVEL GUIDES

COLORADO

BY ANN HEINRICHS • ILLUSTRATED BY MATT KANIA

The Child's World®
childsworld.com

Published by The Child's World®
1980 Lookout Drive • Mankato, MN 56003-1705
800-599-READ • www.childsworld.com

Photo Credits
Photographs ©: iStockphoto, cover, 1; Wasif Malik CC2.0,
7; Greg Hamilton CC2.0, 8; Marianne Tucker/National
Park Service, 11; James St. John CC2.0, 12; National Park
Service, 15, 16; Brady-Handy Photograph Collection/
Library of Congress, 18, 21; Carol M. Highsmith Archive/
Library of Congress, 19, 24; Gary C. Caskey/UPI/
Newscom, 20; Gates Frontiers Fund Colorado Collection/
Carol M. Highsmith Archive/Library of Congress, 23; J.
Raley/AI Wire/Newscom, 27; Paul L. McCord Jr. CC2.0,
28; RiverNorthPhotography/iStockphoto, 31, 32; National
Institute of Standards and Technology, 35; Shutterstock
Images, 37 (top), 37 (bottom)

ISBN 9781503819467
LCCN 2016961123

Printing
Printed in the United States of America
PA02334

post card

Ann Heinrichs is the author
of more than 100 books
for children and young
adults. She has also enjoyed
successful careers as a
children's book editor and
an advertising copywriter.
Ann grew up in Fort Smith,
Arkansas, and lives in
Chicago, Illinois.

About the Author
Ann Heinrichs

post card

Matt Kania loves maps and, as a
kid, dreamed of making them. In
school he studied geography and
cartography, and today he makes
maps for a living. Matt's favorite
thing about drawing maps is
learning about the places they
represent. Many of the maps
he has created can be found in
books, magazines, videos, Web
sites, and public places.

About the
Map Illustrator
Matt Kania

*On the cover: Colorful flowers bloom in spring
near the Colorado Rocky Mountains.*

OUR COLORADO TRIP

COLORADO

re you ready for a tour of Colorado? There's plenty to see and do there! You'll climb steep cliffs and pan for gold. You'll watch machines making money. You'll see dinosaur footprints and see an old trading fort. And you'll hear elks making a terrible racket! Just follow the dotted line. Or make your own tour by skipping around. Either way, you're in for a great ride. Are you all buckled up? Then we're on our way!

WELCOME TO
COLORADO

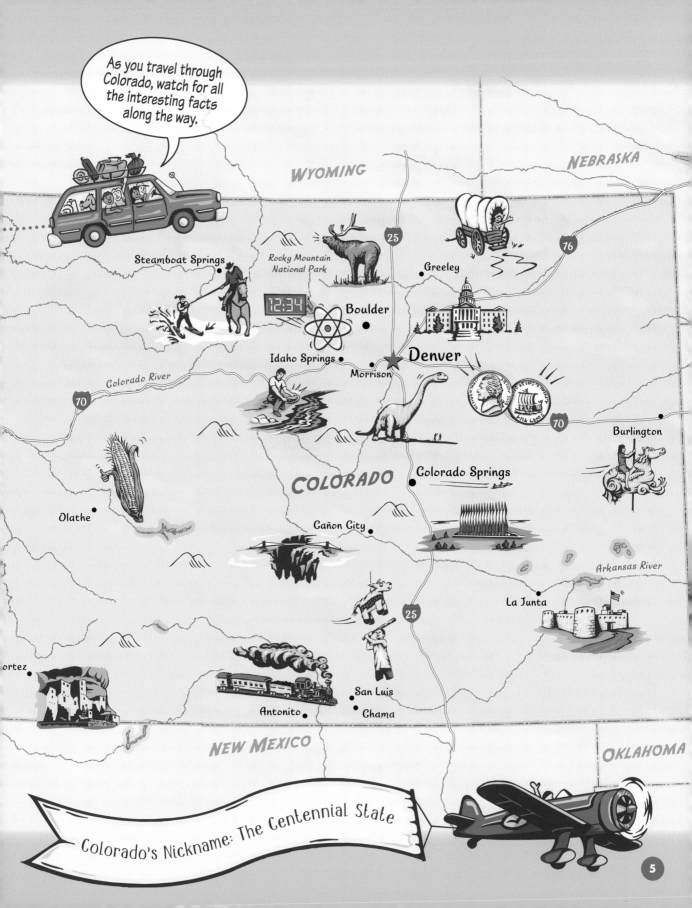

ROYAL GORGE BRIDGE AND THE ROCKY MOUNTAINS

Go ahead and jump! Now you're free-falling high above the river!

That's what the Royal Rush Skycoaster ride is like. It's at the Royal Gorge Bridge near Cañon City. This bridge is in the foothills of the Rocky Mountains. It connects one side of a canyon to another. Far below is the Arkansas River.

The Rocky Mountains run down the middle of Colorado. They're called the Rockies for short. Many people live at the eastern foot of the Rockies. Colorado's biggest cities are there.

West of the Rockies, the land is hilly. It's good for farming and grazing animals. Eastern Colorado is part of the Great Plains. Lots of farming goes on there, too.

You can ride in a gondola across the canyon if you're not afraid of heights!

THE WINTER CARNIVAL IN STEAMBOAT SPRINGS

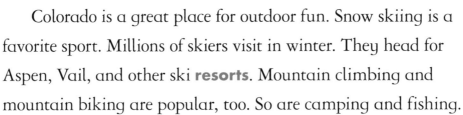

Swoosh! You're sailing down the street on skis. A horse is pulling you along. He pulls you up onto a ramp. Now how far can you jump?

This is a skiing contest called the donkey jump. (There's no donkey—just a horse.) It takes place at the Winter Carnival in Steamboat Springs.

Colorado is a great place for outdoor fun. Snow skiing is a favorite sport. Millions of skiers visit in winter. They head for Aspen, Vail, and other ski **resorts**. Mountain climbing and mountain biking are popular, too. So are camping and fishing.

Try the donkey jump at the Steamboat Springs Winter Carnival, and see how high you can fly!

WYOMING

NEBRASKA

The first public library in Colorado opened in Denver in 1860.

• Steamboat Springs

★ Denver

• Vail

Let's do the donkey jump and the shovel race! And Spot can sign up for the dog dash!

• Aspen

• Telluride

Colorado Sports Teams
Colorado Avalanche (hockey)
Colorado Rapids (soccer)
Colorado Rockies (baseball)
Denver Broncos (football)
Denver Nuggets (basketball)

Steamboat Springs is called Ski Town USA. It has sent more athletes to the Winter Olympic Games than any other U.S. city.

EW MEXICO

Telluride holds a bluegrass music festival every June.

NOISY ELK IN THE ROCKIES

What's that racket? A siren? A trumpet? You're in Rocky Mountain National Park. And that sound is just an elk.

Elk are a type of deer. Autumn is their mating season. The males call out to find a mate. Their call is really loud!

Elk, deer, and moose live in the Rockies. So do bears, bobcats, and bighorn sheep. Antelopes and prairie dogs live on the plains.

Forests cover Colorado's mountains and hills. Spring is a colorful season. Wildflowers bloom across the meadows and hillsides.

Elk often live high up in the Rockies. They move to meadows during mating season.

DINOSAUR RIDGE IN MORRISON

What is on that rock? It looks like large footprints. Who made all these footprints? Giant chickens? No! Dinosaurs made them millions of years ago.

You are walking on the Dinosaur Ridge Trail in Morrison. There are more than 300 dinosaur footprints here! You'll also see dinosaur bones along the trail.

Many dinosaurs used to live in this area. It is mountainous today. But about 100 million years ago, it was a sandy beach. Rivers flowed into an ocean. Many dinosaurs lived and died near the rivers. Their bones washed downstream. Then sand and gravel covered them up.

These dinosaur footprints were colored in with charcoal so that visitors could better see them.

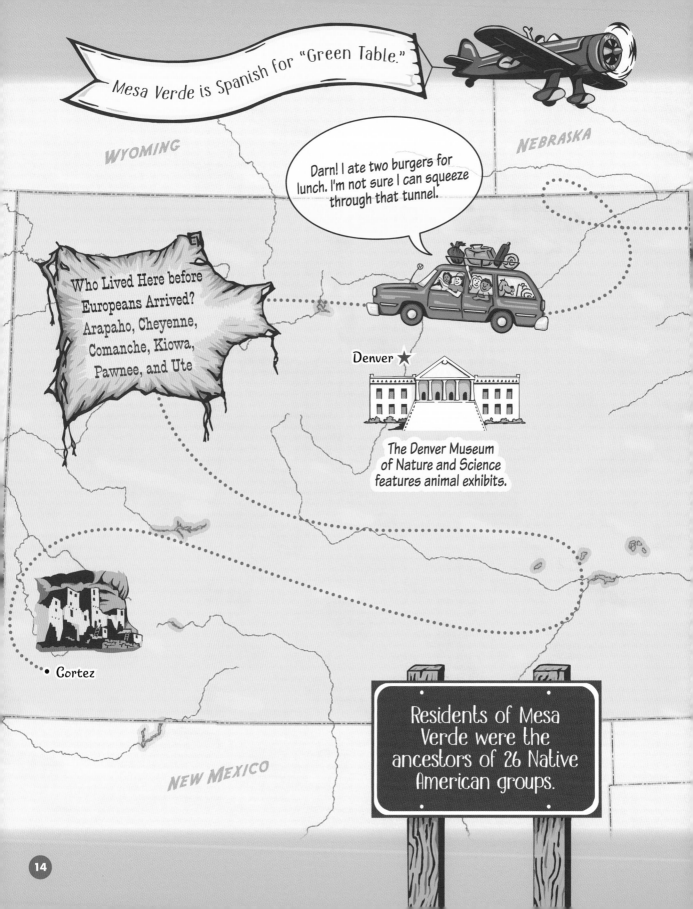

CLIFF DWELLINGS AT MESA VERDE

Climb down the steps. Scramble up a ladder. Crawl through a tunnel. Then climb more steps. Are you worn out yet? You're visiting Balcony House at Mesa Verde, near Cortez.

Mesa Verde was once home to the Pueblo people. These Native Americans lived there more than 1,000 years ago. They built homes and villages in the rocky cliffs. These villages are called cliff dwellings.

The Pueblo people got their water from **springs**. In the 1200s, the springs began to dry up. Then the Pueblo left Mesa Verde. They moved south to present-day New Mexico and Arizona.

Spanish explorers came to Colorado in the late 1500s. They were looking for gold. They didn't find much of it, so they left.

Cliff Palace is the largest cliff dwelling in Mesa Verde. It had 150 rooms!

BENT'S OLD FORT NEAR LA JUNTA

Pick up a barrel of beans. Grab a hatchet or two. Get a buffalo skin while you're at it. That's how people shopped at Bent's Fort. It was like today's convenience store! **Mountain men**, fur traders, and soldiers got supplies there.

The United States gained most of Colorado in 1803. Then U.S. explorers and traders arrived. Many hired Cheyenne and Arapaho people as guides.

Bent's Fort was Colorado's first European settlement. Brothers William and Charles Bent opened it in 1833. Now visitors can tour the rebuilt fort at Bent's Old Fort National Historic Site. They can see how people lived and worked there.

A teepee and a covered wagon outside Bent's Old Fort remind visitors of its past.

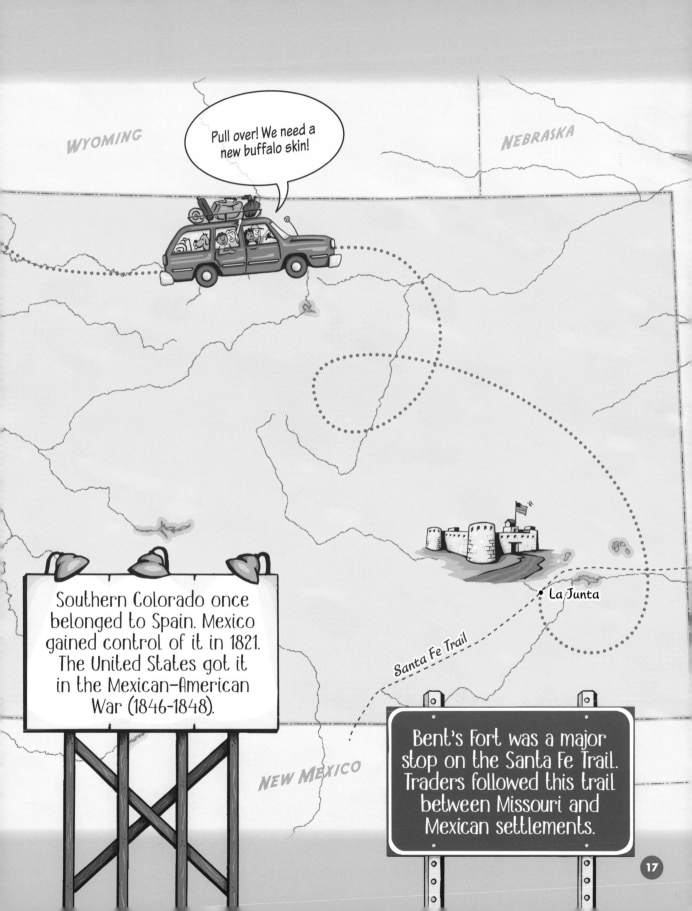

Only about 150 wooden carousels still run in North America.

I want to ride the camel! You take the giraffe! The last one in gets the goat!

WYOMING

NEBRASKA

Dear Mr. Carson:
You were a good hunter. You supplied meat to Bent's Fort. You were a great guide, too. You led settlers along the Oregon Trail. You made sure they got to California and Oregon safely.

Sincerely,
Carol Sell

post card

Mr. Kit Carson
1809-1868
La Junta, CO

Burlington

La Junta

A 1909 Wurlitzer Monster Military Band Organ plays the music as the carousel turns around.

NEW MEXICO

The Kit Carson County Carousel is at the fairgrounds in Burlington.

THE KIT CARSON COUNTY CAROUSEL IN BURLINGTON

Do you like riding **carousels**? Check out the Kit Carson County Carousel. You've never seen anything like it! It has 46 strange animals to ride. You can hop onto goats, lions, giraffes, or camels. There are deer with real antlers. There are horses with actual horsehair tails. All the animals were hand-carved from wood. They were made in 1905.

Kit Carson County was named for Kit Carson. He was a famous hunter, trapper, and guide. Carson knew the Colorado wilderness well.

There are so many choices! Which animal would you want to ride at the Kit Carson County Carousel?

PHOENIX GOLD MINE IN IDAHO SPRINGS

Want some gold? Just head over to the Phoenix Gold Mine. It's in Idaho Springs. You can pan for gold there. Whatever you find, you can keep!

Gold was discovered near Denver in 1858. Suddenly, Colorado had a gold rush. Miners found silver in 1869. Leadville and Aspen became big silver towns.

Miners and farmers poured into Colorado. Sometimes they settled on Native Americans' land. This led to problems between the settlers and the Native Americans.

You need a lot of equipment to mine gold! Tour the Phoenix Gold Mine to learn how it's done.

Dear Mr. Tabor:

You made lots of money mining silver. No wonder people called you the Silver King! Too bad the government stopped buying silver in 1893. You lost your wealth, but you will always be remembered as a hard worker.

Sincerely,
Elizabeth Doe

Mr. Horace Tabor
1830-1899
Denver, CO

WYOMING

NEBRASKA

Logan County

Summit Springs Battlefield is in Logan County. The U.S. Army battled the Cheyenne and Sioux there in 1869.

Here's a tricky question. Which is more valuable—$100 worth of silver or $100 worth of gold?

Denver

Idaho Springs

Aspen •

Leadville

Colorado's Native American wars included the Battle at Milk Creek (1879) in northwestern Colorado.

One of the world's largest silver nuggets was found near Aspen in 1894. It weighed 2,350 pounds (1,066 kg)!

NEW MEXICO

Colorado was the 38th state to enter the Union. It joined on August 1, 1876.

Wow! Really weird stuff happens this high up. Water boils at a lower temperature. And when you throw a ball, it goes farther!

WYOMING

NEBRASKA

★ Denver

Denver was founded in 1859 as a gold-mining camp.

Some people think that Louis Ballast of Denver invented the cheeseburger. He began serving them in his Humpty Dumpty restaurant in 1935.

The tallest building in Colorado is Denver's Republic Plaza. It's 56 stories high.

Welcome to Denver, the capital of Colorado!

Colorado's state motto is "nil sine numine." This is Latin for "nothing without divine will."

THE MILE HIGH CITY

Stroll up to the state capitol in Denver. Go to the steps on the west side. You'll see an engraving on one of the steps. It says, "One Mile Above Sea Level."

Denver is called the Mile High City. Is it really 1 mile (1.6 km) high? Only a couple of spots are. But one is on those steps!

Many state government offices are in the capitol. Colorado's government has three branches. One branch makes the state's laws. It's called the General Assembly. The governor heads another branch. This branch makes sure people obey the laws. The third branch is made up of judges. Judges rule over the courts. They decide if laws have been broken.

The Colorado State Capitol building opened in 1894.

You take your seat in the one-room schoolhouse. You study reading, writing, and arithmetic. Are you behaving yourself? If not, you'll learn how. You also have a class in manners!

You're a student at Lone Valley School. It's at Centennial Village in Greeley. The village explores prairie life in the 1800s and early 1900s.

There are tents and Native American teepees. There are **sod** houses, too. Many early settlers lived in homes such as these.

Some village houses belonged to **immigrants**. Spanish, Swedish, and German settlers built them.

Farmers in Centennial Village used silos like this one to store food for their animals.

In 2016, 5,540,545 people lived in Colorado. It's the 21st-largest state by population.

WYOMING

NEBRASKA

Yum! Tamales are a common food served at the Las Posadas festival.

Denver ★ • Aurora

Colorado Springs •

San Luis is Colorado's oldest town. It was founded in 1851.

Las Posadas takes place nine nights before Christmas. People act out the Bible story of Mary and Joseph's search for shelter before Jesus was born.

San Luis

NEW MEXICO

Population of Largest Cities
Denver.........................682,545
Colorado Springs........456,568
Aurora..........................359,407

LAS POSADAS IN SAN LUIS

A donkey ambles down the street. A girl rides on its back. A boy walks beside it. They are dressed in long robes. You're watching the Las Posadas parade in San Luis. This Mexican festival takes place at Christmastime.

San Luis's first settlers were **Hispanic** people. They moved north from New Mexico. Each Hispanic group has its own special holidays and **traditions**. Many Mexican people in Colorado also celebrate Cinco de Mayo. This Mexican holiday honors Mexico's military victory over French forces on May 5, 1862.

Hispanics are among Colorado's many ethnic groups. Native Americans live in Colorado, too. Nations such as the Cheyenne celebrate the Denver March Powwow. Many Native American groups take part in this gathering.

Hispanic dancers perform during Denver's annual Cinco de Mayo parade.

THE AIR FORCE ACADEMY NEAR COLORADO SPRINGS

Watch those doolies double-timing across the campus! Where in the world are you? At the U.S. Air Force Academy!

Students at the academy are called cadets. First-year cadets are called doolies during basic training. Doolies do a lot of double-timing. That means moving twice as fast as usual!

Colorado grew fast in the early 1900s. New inventions called automobiles were good for the state. Tourists could drive their cars to Colorado. Oil became an important product, too.

Colorado grew even more after World War II (1939–1945). The government opened many centers there. One was the U.S. Air Force Academy.

About 1,400 cadets are accepted into the U.S. Air Force Academy each year.

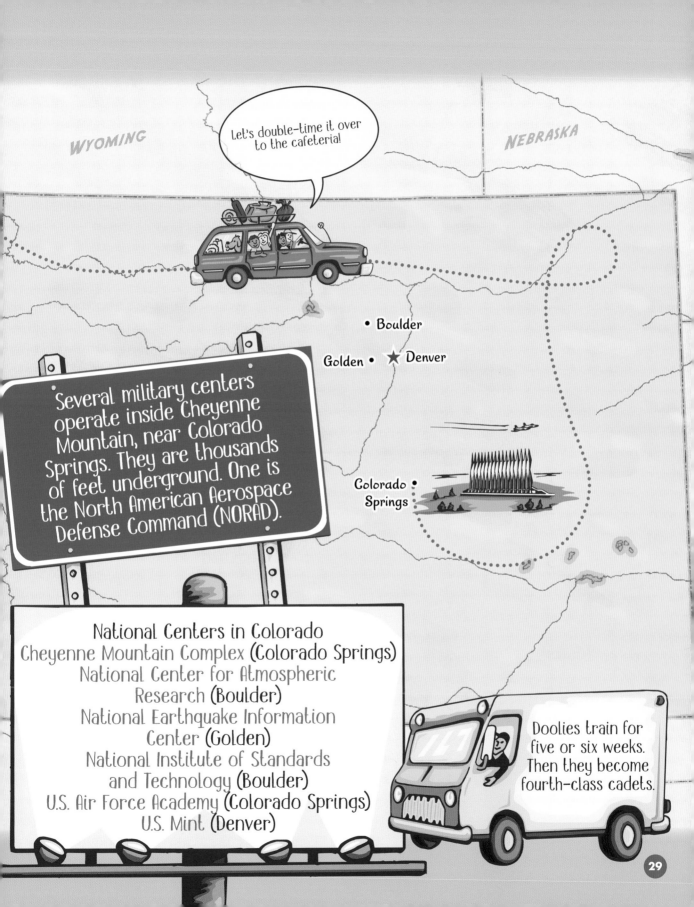

WYOMING

NEBRASKA

Let's double-time it over to the cafeteria!

• Boulder

Golden • ★ Denver

Colorado • Springs

Several military centers operate inside Cheyenne Mountain, near Colorado Springs. They are thousands of feet underground. One is the North American Aerospace Defense Command (NORAD).

National Centers in Colorado
Cheyenne Mountain Complex (Colorado Springs)
National Center for Atmospheric Research (Boulder)
National Earthquake Information Center (Golden)
National Institute of Standards and Technology (Boulder)
U.S. Air Force Academy (Colorado Springs)
U.S. Mint (Denver)

Doolies train for five or six weeks. Then they become fourth-class cadets.

OLATHE'S SWEET CORN FESTIVAL

How much corn can you eat? How far can you spit a corn kernel? There's an easy way to find out. Just stop by the Olathe Sweet Corn Festival!

Corn is Colorado's major crop. Farmers around Olathe grow sweet corn. It's tender and juicy. Yum!

Many farmers raise beef cattle. The cattle graze across wide-open ranges. Later they go to feedlots. There the cattle live in pens. They eat lots of food and gain weight.

More than 60 million pounds (27 million kg) of corn are grown in Colorado each year.

You probably know how to make money. You work hard and earn it, right? Wrong! Well, not in this place, anyhow. It's the U.S. Mint in Denver.

The U.S. Mint is a money factory. It actually manufactures money. It melts metal to make coins. Just take a tour of the mint. You can watch it all happen!

Colorado makes more than just money. Many factories make computers. Others make things to eat and drink. Remember all those beef cattle? Some factories chop up beef and package it.

You'll learn the history of the U.S. Mint and how they make coins when you tour the Denver Mint.

The U.S. Mint makes more than ten billion coins each year.

WYOMING

What's Made in Colorado? Computer and electronic products, food and beverage products, and transportation equipment

What a way to make money! It's a lot easier than mowing lawns.

Denver

One million pennies are worth $10,000.

Pennies are made out of the metals copper and zinc.

What's Mined in Colorado? Coal, natural gas, and petroleum

A coin lasts for about 25 years. Paper money lasts only about 18 months.

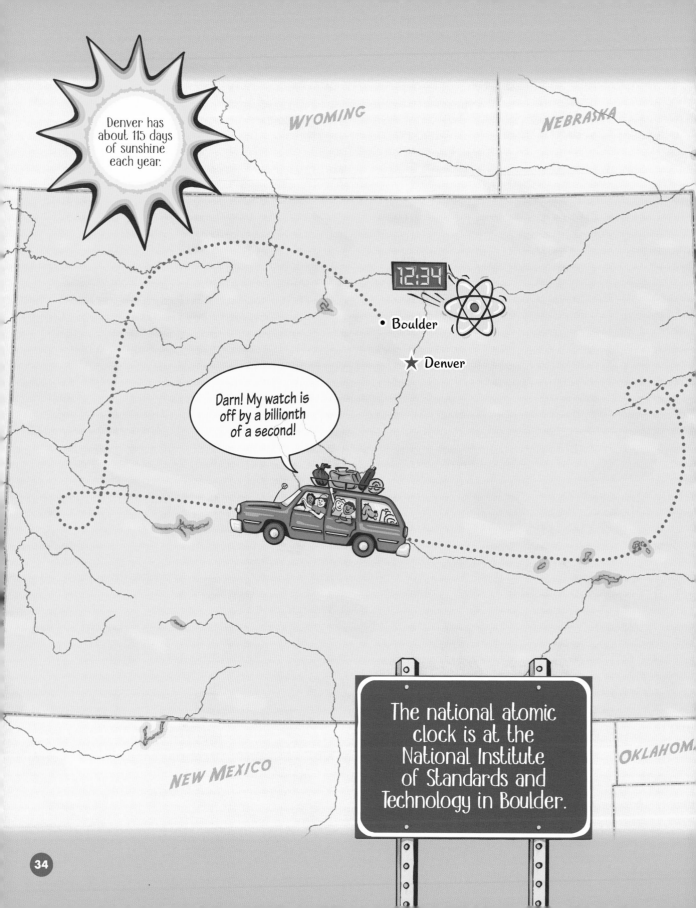

THE NATIONAL ATOMIC CLOCK IN BOULDER

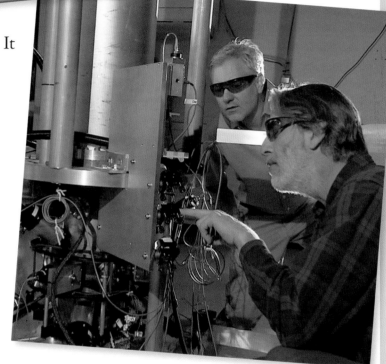

It doesn't go tick-tock. It doesn't even look like a clock. But it's the most important clock in the country. It's the nation's official timekeeper. Its time is the right time!

You can see this famous clock in Boulder. It's an atomic clock. It runs on the energy **atoms** send out.

The atomic clock keeps almost perfect time. How does it do in a week? It won't lose even one-billionth of a second! What if it's still running in 100 million years? It still won't be off by even one full second!

The national atomic clock, or NIST-F2, is no ordinary clock. It uses atoms and lasers to tell time.

OUR TRIP

We visited many amazing places on our trip! We also met a lot of interesting people along the way. Look at the map below. Use your finger to trace all the places we have been.

What is North America's tallest suspension bridge? *See page 6 for the answer.*

How did dinosaur bones become fossils? *Page 13 has the answer.*

Why did the Pueblo people leave Mesa Verde? *Page 15 has the answer.*

How many wooden carousels run in North America? *See page 18 for the answer.*

How much did the huge silver nugget found in Aspen weigh? *Look on page 21 for the answer.*

What is Colorado's oldest town? *Turn to page 26 for the answer.*

How long do doolies train? *Look on page 29 and find out!*

How many coins does the U.S. Mint make each year? *Turn to page 33 for the answer.*

NEBRASKA

WYOMING

25

76

Steamboat Springs

Rocky Mountain National Park

Greeley

12:34

Boulder

Denver

Idaho Springs

Morrison

Colorado River

70

70

Burlington

COLORADO

Colorado Springs

Olathe

Cañon City

Arkansas River

La Junta

25

Cortez

San Luis

Antonito

Chama

NEW MEXICO

OKLAHOMA

STATE SYMBOLS

State animal: Rocky Mountain bighorn sheep

State bird: Lark bunting

State fish: Greenback cutthroat trout

State flower: Rocky Mountain columbine

State folk dance: Square dance

State fossil: Stegosaurus

State gemstone: Aquamarine

State grass: Blue grama grass

State insect: Colorado hairstreak butterfly

State mineral: Rhodochrosite

State tree: Colorado blue spruce

State seal

That was a great trip! We have traveled all over Colorado! There are a few places that we didn't have time for, though. Next time, we plan to ride a train out of Antonito. That's where the Cumbres & Toltec Scenic Railroad is located. We're sure to pass by lovely scenery on our trip!

STATE SONG

"WHERE THE COLUMBINES GROW"
Words and music by A. J. Fynn

Where the snowy peaks gleam in the moonlight,
Above the dark forests of pine,
And the wild foaming waters dash onward,
Toward lands where the tropic stars shine;
Where the scream of the bold mountain eagle
Responds to the notes of the dove
Is the purple robed West, the land that is best,
The pioneer land that we love.

Chorus:
'Tis the land where the columbines grow,
Overlooking the plains far below,
While the cool summer breeze in the evergreen trees
Softly sings where the columbines grow.

The bison is gone from the upland,
The deer from the canyon has fled,
The home of the wolf is deserted,
The antelope moans for his dead,
The war whoop re-echoes no longer,
The Indian's only a name,
And the nymphs of the grove in their loneliness rove,
But the columbine blooms just the same.

Let the violet brighten the brookside,
In sunlight of earlier spring,
Let the fair clover bedeck the green meadow,
In days when the orioles sing,
Let the goldenrod herald the autumn,
But, under the midsummer sky,
In its fair Western home, may the columbine bloom
Till our great mountain rivers run dry.

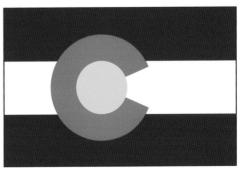

State flag

FAMOUS PEOPLE

Adams, Amy (1974–), actor

Allen, Tim (1953–), actor and comedian

Billups, Chauncey (1976–), basketball player

Carpenter, M. Scott (1925–2013), astronaut

Cech, Thomas R. (1947–), Nobel Prize–winning microbiologist

Denver, John (1943–1997), country/folk singer

Elway, John (1960–), football player

Fairbanks, Douglas (1883–1939), actor

Field, Eugene (1850–1895), children's poet

Ginsberg, Allen (1926–1997), poet

Jackson, William Henry (1843–1942), photographer

Lea, Homer (1876–1912), soldier and author

Lynch, Ross (1995–), actor and musician

McDaniel, Hattie (1895–1952), actor

McKennis, Alice (1989–), Olympic skier

Miller, Glenn (1904–1944), band leader

Mills, Enos (1870–1922), naturalist

Chief Ouray (ca. 1833–1880), Native American chief of the Ute tribe

Robb, AnnaSophia (1993–), actor

Stevens, Janet (1953–), children's author and illustrator

Taylor, Mildred D. (1943–), children's author

Van Dyken-Rouen, Amy (1973–), Olympic swimmer

WORDS TO KNOW

atoms (AT-uhmz) tiny particles of matter

carousels (kar-uh-SELLZ) merry-go-rounds

fossils (FOSS-uhlz) remains or prints of plants or animals that have hardened into stone

Hispanic (hiss-PAN-ik) having roots in a Spanish-speaking land

immigrants (IM-uh-gruhntz) people who leave their home country to settle in a new land

mountain men (MOUN-tuhn MEN) frontiersmen who spent most of their time in the wilderness

nuggets (NUHG-itz) chunks of metal

resorts (ri-ZORTZ) popular places to relax and play

sod (SOD) chunks of soil with grasses and roots attached

springs (SPRINGZ) places where underground water comes to the surface

suspension bridge (suh-SPEN-shuhn BRIJ) a bridge with towers at both ends and a road hanging from cables

traditions (truh-DISH-uhnz) customs and ways of life handed down from generation to generation

TO LEARN MORE

IN THE LIBRARY

Blake, Kevin. *Cliff Dwellings: A Hidden World*. New York, NY: Bearport, 2015.

Kurtz, Jane. *Celebrating Colorado*. Boston, MA: Houghton Mifflin Harcourt, 2016.

Ogintz, Eileen. *The Kid's Guide to Denver, Boulder & Colorado's Ski Country*. Guilford, CT: Globe Pequot, 2014.

Schnobrich, Emily. *Colorado: The Centennial State*. Minneapolis, MN: Bellwether, 2014.

ON THE WEB
Visit our Web site for links about Colorado:
childsworld.com/links

Note to Parents, Teachers, and Librarians: We routinely verify our Web links to make sure they are safe and active sites. So encourage your readers to check them out!

PLACES TO VISIT OR CONTACT
History Colorado Center
historycoloradocenter.org
1200 Broadway
Denver, CO 80203
303/447-8679
For more information about the history of Colorado

Colorado Tourism Office
colorado.com
1625 Broadway, Suite 2700
Denver, CO 80202
303/892-3840
For more information about traveling in Colorado

Colorado covers 104,094 square miles (269,602 sq km). It's the eighth-largest state in size.

INDEX

Bye, Centennial State. We had a great time. We'll come back soon!